AF471924

New Teacher OJT:
What They Don't Teach in School

Donna Burrell

db Professional Solutions

2018

First Printing: 2018

ISBN 978-1-387-87453-8

DB Professional Solutions

Ordering Information:

Special discounts are available on quantity purchases by corporations, associations, educators, and others. For details, contact the publisher at DB Professional Solutions by email: dbprofessionalsolutions@yahoo.com.

Dedication

To Dr. Conner, Dr. Hatton, and Dr. Ford for pushing me to be more than a teacher

Contents

Acknowledgements

I would like to thank many of my coworkers that I worked with throughout the years who were comfortable working with me and following my lead. To the Administrators who empowered me to fill in the gap in the building to keep things going, as well as giving me the keys to sit at the helm in their absences.

Introduction

The formal programs teach and grade rigorously on the ability to create lesson plans, assessments, content and other academic components, but not on the how's and why's of operating in a classroom. The one professor that attempted to tell us some "how to's", would have gotten me and some of my classmates fired, had we done what she suggested. The good thing was that I was already teaching when I was in her class and knew better. We went back and forth for days. When she finally understood that our districts didn't operate the same, the students, communities were polar opposites and the expectations were different, she finally let go. While in class a couple of my classmates chimed in telling her that our district would never require a teacher to do what she suggested and might discipline a teacher if they tried it. Her working in a suburban district created a bias to what happened in other districts. You must gain an understanding of the culture when working within a specific school and/or district, let alone the Principal's expectations and rule of thumb for his/her building.

Unfortunately, most of the learning and experience in these areas doesn't happen until you actually begin your career as a teacher in a school building. School culture varies from building to building within a given district, as well as district to district, even when they are in close proximity of each other, and sharing kids of that area. So once you're years into your career and decide to change schools, remember that what worked in one school may or may not work in another. The varying degrees of differences in schools within a district at the same level is sometimes jaw dropping, despite them have to operate according to the same rules.

Survival in any school is based upon your open-mindedness, willing to learn, ability to adapt and remain flexible because no two days are the same. The ability to get along with key personnel in a school will be your saving grace and reduce any added stress that comes along with your job. Remember, your success depends on the success of your students. And that will come when you remember that it's ok to ask for help. It also includes accepting the fact that you don't know it all, your students are not widgets or robots, and to balance your work and personal life.

Chapter 1: Teaching Is Hard

You're A Student Too

We've all seen others teach and they make it look easy. I can think of a few of my teachers and professors that I thought, "I want to be like her". One specifically, she was my Humanities professor during my undergrad degree. She was tall and lean, confident, very well versed and commanded respect just by her presence. I was talking to my old classmate Perry about her the other day and I told him, she inspired and scared me at the same time. I will never forget Dr. Mays.

I remember the week leading up to the start of the school year, I was sitting and thinking, well telling myself, "You have to watch your mouth, these are kids." I know that I am an aggressive, strong-willed, confident person who speaks her mind and in some instances and/or places, it's not received well or my character and/or personality is misconstrued. I'm just usually passionate about what I do. I keep a stern look on my face (it's kind of natural) and it's not because I'm mean or anti-social or anything, actually I'm the opposite once you get to know me. But the initial reaction from most I encounter is just that. I knew I would rub some the wrong way because of it. And of course I did. Coming to the education industry after 15 plus years in Corporate America, where I had to take a stance to be taken seriously in my jobs/career in the accounting field. I thought my structured way of doing things would be perceived negatively so I consciously worked on my stance, only to realize once I began to teach, it was revered.

I worked in the inner city, by choice, and 90 percent of my students welcomed the structure and expectations that enveloped my room. I would overhear students tell other students, "She's not mean, you just can't come in her room and do what you want." It made me realize that I had to be myself too, so that the students got to know and build a rapport and/or relationship with the real me.

Knowing your content well is only half the battle of being a good teacher. You can have a "Gold Star" lesson plan, but if you're not ready for the unexpected, well, it can be derailed in the first five minutes. If you do not have a plan B or plan C, can't regroup on the fly, you will spend much of the time trying to figure out what to do next, or end up doing something totally different and unrelated to your original lesson.

> Scenario 1: You've prepared all of the materials, have your copies ready, have the room set up exactly the way you want it for the lesson, brought in extra supplies to make sure everyone has what they need to be successful in the lesson…but only half of your class shows up that day.

First thought is, "I need everyone in class to do this, I don't want to repeat all of this and/or have to do it again and lose the students that are here now, when I do". What do I do? How do I engage the few students that are here? Do I punish them for being in class and make them hear it again tomorrow, when I hope the whole class will be present?

> Scenario 2: You have all of your materials ready, handouts set to give students to follow along, and supplies on hand for everyone to participate…and your technology doesn't work.

You attempt to fix it on your own and yet nothing works. It's now 10 minutes into the class so you call the IT person in your building but they're tied up preparing computers for testing. What do you do? Are you prepared to present without the technology? Do you have alternate technology to use? What's your plan B or Plan C?

A great teacher plans for the possibility of something going wrong. If it doesn't, then great. The fact that we're working with people and not widgets, there's always an opportunity for something to throw the plan off course. It could be an unannounced fire drill, other crisis drills, a parent, a sick student, other school based personnel, the possibilities are limitless. I recommend always having a shortened assignment related to that "Gold Star" lesson plan that can be used as an introduction to that lesson. It can be a short discussion about it to determine prior knowledge or a simple pre-assessment to help you decide if you need to tweak the lesson before presenting to the entire class. This is sometimes a blessing in disguise.

The second recommendation is to prepare them for the lesson. If you begin this "Gold Star" lesson and none of your students can relate to the topic, vocabulary or engage in the discussion, you now have a derailed lesson. You will spend more time working on understanding, trying to use analogies to get them to relate to the topic, and maybe some students losing all focus and creating a disturbance that derails any teaching. It's impossible to be prepared for every scenario, but it is easy to ensure they know what they are about to engage in, to keep the classroom conducive to learning.

My normal routine at the beginning of the year for seating in my classroom was to let them sit where ever they landed. I would tell them that where they are is where they're expected to be for the remainder of the school year. A few would ask to change and I would allow it. I would explain that I would use their seats to learn their names and who they are, BUT, if it becomes a problem I would then choose their seat. And if there were multiple seats that became an issue, I would then create a seating chart because now I have watched them long enough to know who shouldn't be near each other. My line to them was, "I don't do seating charts, this is high school, but if you need help doing what's expected, I will decide where you sit." Many would say, "Oh, I'm good, you won't get any problems out of me." I would always just chuckle because those are the ones that usually ended up moving near my desk.

We all know that one size does NOT fit all. And as a teacher, you have to get to know your students because what works with one student may not work for others. I've always had one student that required me to go extra steps in teaching, discipline, word choice and demeanor. Sometimes it was intentional on their part, other times, it was just what was needed to keep order in teaching and learning. Also, if you happen to teach high school, each class period will have a different culture amongst them. Rules and order should be the same but the way it's carried out may be different, only because of the combination of the personalities in the room, as well as the relationships of the class. There will be classes that you will have the most awesome time teaching and engaging with and then there will be others that will feel like pulling teeth from a running elephant. They will require more of you, so be prepared in your planning.

There will be some days you love your job and working with kids and some that you wish you could have total silence. The key is being able to get over or past the feeling that has you in a funk. I played smooth jazz in the background in my classroom. Having this background sound gave me something to pull on and help me fix my mood and be able to regroup to be and do what was expected of me. And it quieted my students. Despite their initial grumble about the music, when it would stop, they would let me know to start it again. I learned that most of my students as well as myself, had a hard time concentrating in total silence. We know that most homes do not operate in silence and they are used to noise, so to have them work in complete silence presented issues with them being focused. I remember having the television and radio playing in our home when I did my homework.

Donna Burrell

It's Okay To Be Human: Take yourself into the classroom

I remember hearing some of the weirdest beliefs that students had of their teachers. Many thought we had to work into the evening because we were always there well after their leave the building. Or that we didn't have any family because we said we were up late working on lesson plans or grading papers. They didn't know that these were the sacrifices that went into being prepared and being a good teacher.

I remember one day I was just sluggish and trying to stay upbeat while teaching and one of the students finally said, "Ms. B., you ok, you don't look good." I told the class that I was tired from being up working on lesson plans and my daughter was sick. Immediately, the students started looking at each other and I could hear them saying, "I didn't know she had kids." Well, needless to say everything took a turn because they had many questions. I answered most, personal ones I would just say next.

From this, I learned to bring myself into the classroom. Being secretive just gives them more of a need to learn about you. I started doing ice breakers and trust building activities on the first days of school. One activity that I did with every class was Name Connect. I would write Ms. Burrell in the middle of the board and a student who could use one of the letters to connect their name to mine would write theirs going down, sort of like a crossword puzzle. After connecting their name they would share something about themselves that you couldn't look at them and know. Such as being a twin, playing musical instruments, writes poetry, etc. My sharing with them made them feel included. This was also powerful because they opened up and I could use their interests and other information in lessons and projects during the year.

What it really does, is show that you are human and have family and issues just as they do in their homes. Since I taught high school I would let them know that I understood that things happen and it may affect their being able to focus and learn. I kept an empty desk or six foot table in my room so that they would have a place to retreat to when necessary. I told them that I understand that things happen out of their control, whether the night before, at home before school or on their way to school, that may put them in a bad place by the time they got to school. I explained that I don't want details but they could take the time to regroup if necessary to be able to engage with the class. Many would come in and point at the table and I would just nod giving them the okay to go to it first. They understood that if they stayed the entire class period they would be responsible for making up the work for that day. Many appreciated the opportunity and that allowed me to build a rapport with them because I gave them a chance to deal with their issue and prepare to learn, without be scolded for not being mentally ready to learn.

It is okay to tell your students about your family. This allowed them to understand and accept your change in mood or demeanor because they know that you have a family and have things happen just as they do. When knowing that you have a family, and you are able to tell them that you are a little tired because of a sick family member or you were out at practices or games, late, so you need them to bear with you for the day. Many of them will respect that. It's also a conversation piece that will allow a common ground to discuss besides academics. Many times students have to work their way into their participation and if there is something that everyone can relate to non-academically, you now have their attention and can transition in to the academics. Other things that you can share are hobbies and sports. I am an alumni of the district that I taught in so I always had stories or events that took place when I was in high school that would help them get through some of the things that they have encountered, or help them prepare for upcoming things. It was a great way to show them that I have been where they are and that I understand fully, what they are going through. And oddly enough, many times they would remind me of things that I may have mentioned that I needed to tend to or do, that were non-school related.

Teacher vs Friend

I have witnessed many teachers who started out being friends with their students only to have a hard time when it came to redirection and discipline. There is nothing wrong with being friendly and empathetic with your students but there must be boundaries to keep the teacher-student relationship pure. Once the student believes or feels that they are above the classroom rules or expectations, you will begin to lose your authority in the room with them and the rest of the students. This will also cause confusion amongst the students when they see what may be considered as favoritism. You will have great relationships with some and never have to have the talk, and others you may never connect with, and that's okay.

The first three days of school I spent a lot of time emphasizing my classroom expectations, which they all received on paper and signed acknowledging that they read it. I talked about how the class would run, the syllabus and how once everyone could follow the rules, respecting me and any adult in my place, each other and their property, we would be able to enjoy and have fun while learning and working together. When the boundaries are set on day one you have less instances of having to stop teaching to address the bad behaviors. Being fair and consistent will create a room/class that will hold each other accountable, and in some cases, they will remind you of the rules and you owning the responsibility of what you said and implemented.

Learn To Let Go

Dealing with people, you will always have the opportunity for disagreements and misunderstandings. It's no different when working with children, no matter the age. Some will not like you for whatever reason, and that is not your problem. You may remind them of someone who was not pleasant to or with them, or they feel did them wrong. I reminded one kid of his mother and another of her aunt, so there was always some type of tension. But what I did not do, was feed into it. My number one reason for interaction was teaching and learning. And once they saw that I wouldn't waiver on that, it diminished and we were able to get through class without incident.

Should there be an incident that results in negative words, having to have them removed from class, suspended or any other discipline, YOU MUST LEARN TO LET GO. It may be difficult in the beginning but I promise you, if you hold onto a grudge, constantly reminding the student of the incident, or continue to bring it up in the classroom, you will suffer more than that student. Most kids will move on in time and so must you. It becomes unnecessary stress and it will hold you back from being the great you that you can be, mentally. You will start with the, I wish he/she wasn't here, I'm not in the mood and all these other thoughts that will take you away from engaging your students and being present in the room at that time. This will create other issues because your mood is tense. You may react or interact with other students improperly. Now you have more to deal with that doesn't involve teaching.

Kids are very sensitive today. Many at no fault of their own as they are dealing with traumas on their own, in living situations that are not the best, whether it's foster care, a group home or living with other family members. Many want to escape these things, and for some, it's when they're at school that they can be a kid and deal with normal kid stuff. So learn not to take everything personal. Teaching requires a thick skin because you will get dumped on mentally, without fail. I will talk about compassion fatigue later. What's projected onto you may have absolutely nothing to do with you.

You Get What You Expect

I have seen many teachers and professors blatantly tell a student that they didn't expect much from them despite not knowing the student's work ethic or personal regard for their education. This is the worst thing you can do as a teacher. This mentality and verbiage will cause a student to give you just what you expect. And if you are negative in dealing with a student regarding their ability to be successful in your class, they will almost surely give you just that, nothing.

If you start your class with the expectation that everyone can learn and will be successful and relay that to them, they will actually work to that expectation. No one wants to fail on purpose, that I've encountered, anyway. And if you hold them accountable when and if they start to fall behind, it will give them the opportunity to catch up and do their part. There's nothing like having someone to believe in you to fuel your own fire to be successful.

Also, being respectful with your students is a must. The old authoritarian or dictatorship run classroom of, "I'm the adult in the room you will respect me", does not work with the students of today. We have all been taught that respect goes both ways, and it's no different in the classroom. Just because they are young or young adults does not mean that they deserve any less when it comes to respect. On the first days of school I told my students that respect goes both ways and I will be respectful to and with them and expect it in return, as well as for any other adult that's in the room with or for me.

If you happen to let your biases and stereotypes control you, you will have continuous battles while trying to teaching. I've seen and heard teachers demean the very students they are there to teach. Most of them will pick up on your ill feelings toward them and may actually say something about it. If you have an issue with a certain ethnic group then teaching in certain areas may not be for you. You should make sure that you don't put yourself where you can only tolerate them and not be sincere in working with them. It's not fair to the students and you will be creating extra stress that will most definitely cause early burnout if not disciplinary actions.

I have encountered many who have had the idea that they would come to a certain area to save the kids. Your job is to teach them. The mentality of they need help will set up a situation of resentment and uncooperativeness. Your looking down on them, that they need saving instead of being taught, can be counterproductive. You must find a way to relate to them, not point out what they lack, what they need to do or determine what's best for them, that is not our job as an educator. If you can't find a way to relate to and with them, you won't be able to educate them.

When I began teaching I remember always hearing, find a way to relate your curriculum to their everyday lives. If there are cultural differences, it is your responsibility to find a way to make the lessons relatable. You can enlist their opinions on upcoming assignments and projects, especially since they have to do the work. You can talk with school support staff or other educators. But whatever you do, do not use anything that can be misconstrued as race specific. In some instances it is okay but there is a fine line for that to get misinterpreted.

When engaging your students ensure that you can speak their language. And that they can understand yours. Many lessons and relationships have been wrecked due to verbiage. If you talk to them in your language and don't explain any words that may seem to go over their heads, you will cause them to disengage. And if they ask you to clarify, please do. Understanding your words as it relates to the lesson will either engage or disengage them. Should you lose them due to not explaining things they're having trouble with, you will spend more time trying to get that lesson going and possibly create behavioral issues because they aren't engaged anymore. Remember, they are there to learn and new words can be the beginning. It's very okay to teach things that aren't in the book. I believe that teaching the "whole child" is a much better concept than just forcing academics on them.

Discipline

During my time as a teacher I had few problems with discipline. Part of that is due to my natural demeanor. This prevented disruptions while I was teaching. I also believe that going over my expectations and class rules (many aligned with school rules) for the first three days along with creating a democratic classroom, curtailed much of the bad behaviors. Avoid being the authoritarian or dictator type teacher. Students will attempt to challenge it often.

You have to remember that many of your students despite their age are doing many of the things that you do as well. Middle and high school students are sometimes attending school, working jobs, taking care of babies, siblings, parents and grandparents. So they are entering your classrooms with stresses just as you are. Many of the younger children are living with those they'd rather not be with or have parents who may not be giving them the attention they need and deserve.

These things present themselves when they feel they are being called out, picked on or addressed negatively, like yelling at them. Having to deal with these various issues, your tone of voice or misunderstanding of something can be that "thing" that sets them off. Rather than immediately sending them to the office or to be removed, use three or four minutes to try to understand what the root of the problem may be to help them get through it. Many will tell you what they don't like or what makes them upset, escalating their behaviors. And if they do, try to remember it for the future. If it's true and total disrespect, that's a different issue, do what you must to end it. If you're able to get them talking, show some empathy and help them, and also help yourself so that you know how to de-escalate their behaviors should they arise again.

Each student will respond differently so make sure you're not increasing their behaviors or enraging them. If you see that what you're trying to do is not working, stop immediately and find another adult who they may have a relationship with, to help them. And you may become that teacher for/with other students that teachers call upon to help them with a familiar student they can't get through to. I know I had kids daily that weren't mine but I worked well with them. I didn't mind if it was going to help them reengage in school. And that's not something that every teacher will take upon themselves to do, and that's fine if it's not you. Just remember, everyone needs help some time.

Parents

Despite many of the things you may hear or see and the stereotypes you see in the news or on social media, most parents want the best for their child(ren). They want to be involved and know how they are doing. Some are just as temperamental as their kids, so you may also have to find someone who has a rapport with them to get through to them. But you can also try to build one of your own when they are calm. And please follow whatever instructions you are given by the parent(s) related to dealing with their child that are within reason, of course. Calling them when they've asked you not to can jeopardize employment or other things as well as create more tension with the family, destroying the parent-teacher relationship.

Also, make sure you do your part and reach out to parents early if there are issues. And if they are academic, please do not wait until it's time for progress reports or report cards to inform them about their student falling behind or failing. Give them the opportunity to help and if they don't, you've done your part in being proactive to include them. Being prepared for parent-teacher conferences is also a must. A parent doesn't only want to hear negative things about their student. Find a way to point out any shortcomings with a positive solution.

Offer them a way to help their student get back on track if they have fallen behind or are failing a course. It's easy to point out problems but offering a solution makes it that much more bearable.

Chapter 2: Key Personnel

Principal

Principals operate as the chief education officer of its school. They are tasked with providing leadership in collaboration with the Superintendent and other designated personnel for the development, implementation and continuous evaluation of a school improvement plan. They are to supervise all supporting services in the school to include Special Education, after-school programs, discipline programs, etc. They are required to implement and enforce all policy, procedures and administrative rules and regulations. Principals are in charge of collaborating with the district office personnel in developing and adhering to the school budget, observations and evaluations of teaching staff, oversee the upkeep of the building while creating a learning culture for its student body.

Principals are also tasked with building community within the neighborhood in which they're located and working with the local business community to gain resources, tangible and intangible. Working with local business partners has grown to help students prepare for the real world through program offerings, technical support of business personnel within the school, internships for students and the ability to gain college credit with local trade colleges.

Head Secretary

The person in this position is the backbone of the school. She knows everything that the Principal does as everything goes through them. They are the direct line to the Principal and the operation of the school. They should be your first line of contact when wanting to reach out to the Principal. They will give you the insight necessary on how to proceed with your request. Befriending the person in this role will help your time in that school be that much easier on you. Not only are they the right hand of the Principal, they are very knowledgeable of everything that goes on in the school. They understand and assist on working on the budget, processes payroll, in charge of building keys, personnel paperwork, and setting up class coverage when teaching staff is out.

If you need to have a conversation with the Head Secretary, please do not attempt to do so at the beginning of the day when staff is checking in or at the end of the day during student pick up time. This should only happen if it affects the day. Honestly, informing them of any changes or needs should happen before the day it is needed. Except for emergencies of course. Preplanning is key for things to flow smoothly. The office is hectic at these times and their attention is focused on getting the day off to a smooth start and any emergencies. Any requests that you have are best submitted in writing so that they can forward it to the necessary personnel if needed. This prevents them from having to disturb you during class if other information is needed. Also, if you are requesting to talk with the Principal regarding an issue, make sure that you are including how you can help rather than just to complain. That will be stopped in its tracks as they have enough to deal with, internally and externally. I have assisted in the office on many occasions and there are very few quiet moments as calls are coming in, students are coming in, parents and district are doing both. My advice is to plan accordingly, as much as possible.

Keys

The keys assigned to you should be guarded just as those for your personal life. Students should not have access to your keys and ensure that you follow whatever the school policy is for keys. A lost key can cause a Principal thousands of dollars should it go missing. Entire schools have had to be rekeyed due to lost keys. Many open multiple doors and should you have the opportunity to have any sort of master key, it getting into the wrong hands can create many issues. Following the policy also prevents any extra stress should you call out and the keys are needed for the substitute taking your place. Yes there are other keys, but sometimes depending on a particular room, there may be supply closets, cabinets and other keys to things in the room that are only on your key ring. I covered a class for a science colleague and the lesson required supplies that were in the cabinets. Well needless to say, no one had the keys to the cabinets and the teacher did not leave there keys so I had to improvise on the lesson, on the fly. I'm no science teacher so with the help of the class, we got through the hour. To avoid creating extra work for substitutes and administration, or any disciplinary actions or unwanted discussions, adhere to the policy given to you. If there are situations that warrant you needing your keys, make sure you talk with the Head Secretary in advance so that everyone is aware of what's taking place. Explaining after the fact could place you in a bad situation.

Calling Out

Even though we're expected to be at work each day, absences are inevitable. Family emergencies, illnesses of self and family, and the need of mental health days will occur. And if you're sick, rather than expose your students and the staff, staying home until you're healthy is preferred. Following protocol is necessary to reduce stress for the staff in attendance. We know emergencies will happen, but if you have to be off, and know in advance, planning with the Head Secretary is recommended. It will allow her the time needed to get coverage of your classes or students that will cause the least disruption of the day.

If teaching in high school there are more staff to choose from to help with coverage of your classes, but in the elementary schools, it's a lot more complicated if the school isn't able to get a substitute. Unfortunately, there is a shortage of substitutes just as there is for teachers. Especially during certain times of the year. There seems to be certain times of the school year that more people out at the same time or if an illness is plaguing the building, such as the flu, colds, etc. And as we will need someone to cover our classes when necessary, when asked to cover for others, it's only fair to help out. No one likes to give up their free or planning time, but being a team player will be remembered.

Assistant Principal

The Assistant Principal(s) within the school have various roles and duties within the school. Most are responsible for student discipline. In some districts/schools, this may be their only responsibility, but most will take on other duties. They are responsible for student monitoring, creating behavior plans with students and their parents/guardians when necessary. They also represent the school during district level suspension hearings. Many Assistant Principal's, take a leadership role according to the school's succession plan for the Principal in their absence.

Many are responsible for teacher observations and evaluations, in charge of transportation if it's provided to students, scheduling/master schedule of classes, and extracurricular activities such as sports teams and are responsible for the building during its use for after school activities. As they have many roles working internally with the school they are also responsible with some of the external functions of the school to include building community relationships with the neighborhood families as well as the business community.

Head Custodian

The person in this role is responsible for the upkeep of the building inside and out, and the personnel in their department. Many think they are there just to clean and that's furthest from the truth. They are responsible for the aesthetics of the building, timing of clean up after lunch hours, and building maintenance. They answer to the Principal as well as the district's facility office.

Many times the things that seem to be simple to get fixed may be just that, but in most buildings, they are required to put in a work order to get it done if the work is under a certain union base and are not allowed to fix it themselves. Unfortunately, in large districts, what the school personnel may consider to be an emergency, may not be at the next level, or it just may take some time for that particular work group to be able to get to your issue. I have seen an emergency work order put in and it take almost two weeks before someone could come to the building. So although it is important to you in your room, on the scale of what is going on in the building, it may not be high on the list of what's attended to.

If it's something that you can do yourself or with a coworker, maybe you should ask them if it's ok to do it yourself along with the approval of someone in Administration. And if you're told it has to be done by the Head Custodian or their personnel, please don't disregard that. This is another issue that can cause more unnecessary stress.

School Leadership/Learning Team

This team is made up of administration personnel, department chairs, reading specialist, curriculum specialist, assessment coordinators, guidance counselors, parent coordinators and sometimes the school social worker and psychologist if on staff. This team is responsible for the School Improvement Plan (SIP). If there is something that you believe should be discussed that is an issue for more than yourself, you have an idea or solution that you feel would benefit the school, taking it to one of these members with a full proposal can be shared with the whole team to determine next steps, if any.

Meetings occur by discipline, across grades and sometimes cohorts. Meeting schedules are usually shared in the organization days prior to school starting. Your attendance is expected and most often required as part of your teacher day. The information that's discussed at the leadership/learning team meetings is then brought to the subcommittee meetings to ensure that everyone is aware of what's going on, expected to be done or needs to take place, with the timeline for completion. And the information from the subcommittees is brought back to the leadership/learning team to inform them of what's being done to reach the set goals of the plan.

Chapter 3: Politics

Unfortunately, politics will always exist in education just as any other entity. Due to public education having so many stakeholders inside and outside of the schools/districts, it's wise to learn to know when to share your opinions. This is not to say that you should not have one or express it, but be mindful of with whom and where you do. There will be internal politics as well. Again, choose wisely on what you involve yourself with. In some cases it becomes more draining and stressful than helpful.

We all have our beliefs about education and what should be done to improve it within our schools, cities and the nation overall. Having to deal with politicians and other outside stakeholders who may not have a clue as to what really takes place, doesn't stop them from making decisions that affect us and our students. And with that, learning to operate within these parameters is very key.

You will be expected to work within the culture, being the best you. There will be times you disagree with certain rules, decisions, outcomes, assigned duties, classes and more, but it is best that you find a way to work within the parameters that have been set without causing waves. It's great to have opinions and ideas, but how they are presented will make all the difference. Openly displaying your feelings against these things can show your unwillingness to be a team player. Despite your personal feelings toward any of this, there is a way to address them. If something bothers you that much, ask for a sit down with your boss. You may learn the whys or rationale behind many of the decisions. Now there will be times that you won't get an answer that you like, because it may be just what is necessary to run the school efficiently.

Understanding how things are done within a particular school is your responsibility to learn. There will be things that are different from what you may have learned in school or heard from other teachers. You have to ask questions and gain an understanding to be successful within that school. Although Principals of a district answer to the same rules and regulations, each school will be run according to that Principal's beliefs, experiences, student population and community in which it is located.

The Glee Club

I use this term to describe the different cliques that exist or that will form by the staff within the school. I've always been good at making friends or just striking up a conversation with anyone, but I don't like being part of a group that demeans others because they can. First of all, it's unprofessional and these biases will get in the way of doing your job and/or objectively working with others. I have seen it ruin careers because someone believed what was told to them and it wasn't the truth.

What was a bit offsetting was seeing the behaviors of adults who resembled the kids that we were there to teach. I learned the hard way to be cordial, participate in what I thought was good fit for me and to mind my business. Many times I would not leave my room other than to go to the restroom, the office or a meeting. Participating in these behaviors serves no one any good. And do know that the students pick up on these behaviors and will comment if they have heard anything, whether good or bad because some teachers were bold enough to talk ill of another teacher in the presence of students. That to me is very childish, unprofessional and exemplifies misconduct.

Be conscious of the relationships that you build. Work to build those that will assist you in becoming the best teacher you can be and help you grow and spread your wings in the education arena.

Pick Your Battles

There will be occasions where you don't agree with something that has taken place in the school, a decision that was made by administration that involves you, changes in your schedule or even a day. Sometimes it's done purely for efficiency, other issues that are taking place that you're not privy to know about, or an authoritarian move by the Principal. Whichever the case may be, standing your ground and voicing your opinion may help and in some instances, may create backlash from those in charge.

If you should disagree with something that involves you personally you are within your right to ask about it, but you should also be prepared to not get an answer that you believe you deserve. Pursing an issue that you feel needs more explaining or prefer a different outcome, can be seen as insubordination, defiance, not being a team player, and place yourself in a position to not receive the help you may need later down the road. It's all about how you present the issue. Make sure that you are talking to someone who has the ability or authority to do something about it. Repeating it over and over to colleagues will give it the opportunity to be told wrong, false information being added and a completely new story when heard by a supervisor. This can only create tension and new issues to be addressed.

Think Before You Speak

We've all been taught this as kids and growing into adulthood. This applies when to talking to students, as well as adults. Once you've said it, there's no taking it back. And depending on your comments, it can be detrimental to your career and growth in the education arena. It can ruin relationships, personal and professional, change someone's perception of you and your abilities, or worth of being part of that school team. I have seen personnel get transferred in the middle of the school year because of their lack of professionalism in talking with someone in administration.

It is imperative to learn to not lash out during tough times, bad situations and moments of anger. We are all human but being able to "bite your tongue" will save you from future confrontations, whether it is with a student, a parent/guardian and/or school personnel. That moment of misspeaking can cause more harm than managing to remain quiet. I believe waiting until you have calmed down to address an issue gives you a chance to think about the entire situation. You can then see if you were a part of the problem, what are the possible solutions and have the ability to speak tactfully with a thought out response.

Other Duties as Assigned

I don't know of any job that does not have this listed as the last item on a job description of responsibilities. Education is no different, it comes with the territory. Students will always need to be monitored or things don't quite go as planned, needing additional personnel. In elementary schools there's lunch room duty, recess duty, bus duty and others that you may get called on to do when a person is needed or to fill in the gap if someone else isn't available. In the middle and high schools there's hall monitoring, attending special meetings, chaperoning events during school hours, providing coverage for others to attend meetings, assisting with testing, IEP meetings and other school specific things.

I've learned that just going with the flow will keep your stress levels down rather than trying to plead your case why you can't or shouldn't, during the time of need. Being a team player is necessary to keep as much efficiency throughout the day as possible. Education is a business of people so there will always be the opportunity for the need to fill in the gap. If it's an after school event, then you should be able to say no, unless it was already relayed to you that it is part of your duties or a requirement of your position. It goes a long way when you can help fill in the gap willingly, without confrontation, or it being a direct order.

Donna Burrell

Chapter 4: Finding Balance

Compassion Fatigue

As a teacher I remember learning about the different issues that my students were faced with and worked to not let it pull on me. It was difficult as many reminded me of my own child or nieces and nephews. It was hard to not internalize their issues because it's hard to watch a child suffer. I remember one young lady (God rest her soul), who would ask me for $2 every day after school. I would always say that I don't have any money. One day one of the teams was selling pizza and soda after school and she asked me to buy some and I told her to eat at home. The next time they announced it, the same thing. Then one day I finally asked her why don't she eat when she gets home, she told me that there wasn't any food at home. I remember blowing it off telling her that she was just trying to get my money. Well, one of my students came to me in class and told me that she's always asking for money because she was telling the truth, that there wasn't any food at their house, hardly ever was. That made my heart sink and I started feeling guilty, what's $2. So if I had it on me when she asked I would give it to her. And there were others, and I had to reign myself in because I would be broke if I helped someone every time they asked, which was often.

Donna Burrell

When I began working in the mental health industry as a Crisis Stabilizer and a Wraparound Care Coordinator, I remember thinking, this is going to be hard. It's so hard not to care when you are placed in the middle of these families as a vital part of the youth's life in helping them deal with their mental health issues. I had cases that ranged from ages 8 – 18. The trauma that they have suffered and continue to work on to just get through the day was overwhelming for me. I remember getting upset, frustrated, thinking somebody needs to pay, all types of emotions that made me work over and beyond. And then it took over and I had to regroup because I had internalized their situations and had a hard time separating. I was able to back up and stick to my job. When you're passionate like I was about helping them deal with their mental health issues, it will get the best of you. I suffered from hair loss and my doctor had to place me on high blood pressure pills because of the stress level that I reached in working with these cases. While trying to help the kids/youth, dealing with the adults was even more stressful because some were in denial, didn't care to help the kid/youth in need and some of the placements were just in it for the money. I had step back and realize that it had gotten the best of me and I needed to leave the position. I realized that I had to find a different way to help them. And that is by helping the adults that will help them. Compassion fatigue is very real and will get you when you least expect it.

Compassion fatigue is described as the physical and emotional exhaustion and profound decrease in the ability to empathize. It is considered to be a secondary form of traumatic stress, as the stress occurs as a result of helping or wanting to help others who are in need. It has been referred to as burnout, but they are not the same. Compassion fatigue is more treatable than burnout, but it can be less predictable and may come suddenly or without much warning. Burnout usually develops over time. (www.lesley.edu)

Many of our students and some of our colleagues are dealing with traumatic experiences. Some have acknowledged them and many have not. A lot of our students have become desensitized to a lot of the tragic things that are happening around them and have never accepted that they have been traumatized. And there are many who have had horrific experiences and are receiving help. Even though there is help, many have yet learned to deal with them in certain settings or with certain people. There are situations that will cause them to act out, need extra attention, only work with certain people, aren't able to adjust to change and many other things that you won't be aware of until there is an incident, drawing you in.

The most common signs and symptoms of compassion fatigue include:

- Chronic exhaustion (emotional, physical or both)
- Reduced feelings of sympathy or empathy

- Dreading working for or taking care of another person and feeling guilty as a result
- Feelings of irritability, anger, or anxiety
- Depersonalization
- Higher sensitivity or complete insensitivity to emotional material
- Feelings of inequity toward caregiver (student/teacher) relationships
- Headaches
- Trouble sleeping
- Impaired decision making
- Weight loss
- Problems in personal relationships
- Poor work-life balance
- Diminished sense of career fulfillment

If you're taking care of someone at home as well as dealing with traumatized students, or your own traumas, you can become more susceptible to compassion fatigue.

Some ways that educators can protect themselves from the possible side effects of working with traumatized students are:

- Get educated
- Practice self-care
- Set emotional boundaries

- Engage in outside hobbies
- Create healthy friendships outside of work
- Keep a journal
- Boost your resiliency
- Use positive coping skills
- Identify workplace strategies
- Seek personal therapy

As an educator is important to know your limitations and how your engaging with traumatized students can affect you personally/mentally, other students in the classroom and your ability to be an efficient teacher. Adhere to the following to help yourself in decreasing stress as well as becoming overwhelmed to the point of needing to deal with trauma yourself.

1. Know what is yours to do.
   Learn how to separate what you wish you can do from what you know you can do. Focus on the task at hand and be present with and for your students. Be mindful of those students and do your part to create a safe room that is conducive to learning for all of your students.
2. Be okay with a different outcome.
   Practice being less attached to exactly how you think things should look or be. Continue to care about your teaching as a craft and the ability to connect with your students, but loosen

the grip on your wanting to control everything. Instead, use humor and compassion which will help you come up with creative solutions.

3. Develop a self-care routine.

   Find times within the day for some quiet alone time to get centered by think about things that make you smile or happy. Adding a balanced diet, getting outside, exercising, dancing, drawing and even coloring can help you relax and refocus. And most of all don't take on more than you know you can do efficiently. It's okay to say no and not feel guilty.

4. Create a strong circle.

   Create a trusted community with your professional colleagues that you can trust where you can share your thoughts, fears, hopes and successes without resentment or repercussions. Work to have someone you can call on when you're in a difficult situation with a student.

5. Be yourself.

   As stated before go into the room as yourself, the true honest you that you know how to be. When you're fully present and being yourself the students build a relationship/rapport with you and it gives them the mind to be the true them as well. It allows you to meet them where they are and work together in growing as a student. It builds trust of you as a teacher as you are giving them who you are and not who think you should be.

6. Work to use mindfulness daily.

> Practicing mindfulness daily will lead to improved memory and focus, better sleep, lower blood pressure, reduced anxiety and depression. For just a few minutes in a day, mindfulness meditation helps create greater empathy, closer connections, and a better sense of well-being. It can also provide a new perspective.

Many companies have begun to include mental health days within the types of time/days off, with pay. If there is no direct title for it, a sick day is a sick day. Take the time necessary to make sure that you are mentally and physically healthy. You are no good to anyone if you are not well yourself. We all have times where we need to regroup and clear our minds to prepare to be a better us. Take that time when and if it presents itself.

Family

Becoming an educator adds your family to the equation. Much of your family life is altered by your career, as you bring work home, have to stay at work late for events, conferences, and not being able to help out around the house. And when you reach burnout at the end of the year, your level of functioning may decrease. Family members may have to double their duties because you're not mentally or physically (unable or not there) able to help out.

This also includes finances since we know that most don't get into the education field for the money. Not being paid for the extra hours that are put into being a good teacher may affect your bottom line. This is something that should definitely be discussed early on in your decision to become a teacher, unless you received money from that proverbial "rich uncle". Plan how you will spend your summer months well in advance so there are no surprises for your family, whether monetary or just being available.

Remember that finding a workable balance between work and family is key. Keeping your stresses at a minimum so that they do not spill over into your work life and vice versa. Plan ahead to not miss the monumental moments of your family members. There's nothing like trying to explain to a child why you aren't able to attend a performance, graduation or other major event.

It's OK To Say No: Avoid Being Voluntold

There's always a need for help or extra hands in every school. And being new, you will be called upon first to jump in and help out, to learn the ropes. You may accept it to appear eager to learn, be helpful, wanting to be a team player, but don't let it set you up for being the go to person every time there is a need. My first years of teaching I was called on for just about everything, mainly because of my previous business experiences. In my second year, one of the guidance counselors saw me in the stair well and asked if I planned on attending the graduation ceremony that evening. I said yes and she replied, "Well, I know that you will be wearing something nice so I will have you read names during the ceremony." I wasn't given a chance to say no, I had been "voluntold". Now I'm not able to change my mind about attending because I'm expected to be there. This changed my whole way of functioning for the evening in less than a minute. This was just one instance of that year. It continued to happen until my Principal told me, "Burrell, you know you can say no, right. You're going to burn out trying to help everyone." And that is when I started saying no to the many request or moments of being voluntold. I was attending night school for my master's degree, my daughter had just started high school, I was running a home based business, as well as teaching.

So stop before you start. Don't say yes when you really mean no. if you say yes and don't come through, it will create last minute issues for whomever is in charge. It will also add to your burnout, offsetting your work-home balance, and overall stress levels. If it's not something you're truly interested in being a part of, let the others take it on. If your hearts not in it, it will definitely feel like work.

Chapter 5: Understanding Culture

When I began teaching I saw many teachers blatantly subject their biases, stereotypes, and beliefs toward the very student they've been tasked with teaching. I began in the math department and was the only Black at the time. It wasn't an issue as I have been in this situation many times. But what was an issue was the disregard, disrespect and name calling from teaching staff for the minority students, they were there to teach.

I have worked in several high schools and each had a majority of an ethnic group while the teaching staff was mostly Caucasian. I have confronted teachers who have shown this disrespect openly and without just cause. To hear them label, stereotype, and demean students because of their ethnicity was unacceptable to me. When you can't separate yourself from what's expected of you, teaching in urban areas may not be for you. I've had co-workers turn their biases on me as well. I used the opportunity to tell them about themselves and the injustice that they were doing to the students that sat in their classes. They weren't aware that I knew what was going on in their classes and I mentioned it to let them know that not everyone was just there for a paycheck. If you can't find a way to be sincere in what you're doing as an educator you are in the wrong field. Students will pick up on your sarcasm, demeaning words and many will call you out for it.

If your personal feelings and opinions dictate your interactions or the lack of, you have to question yourself if you've chosen the right career. If you go in with the thought or believe what you've been hearing and seeing, that the students are "thugs", "those kids", "criminals", and other names that I've heard, you should not work where they are. Not every student you encounter will be what you perceive them to be. Many of them did not ask to be in the life that was handed to them. Their family situations is only one they can live through and change as they get older. They should not be faulted by the decisions made by their parents/guardians.

Educators today hear a lot about gaps in education, achievement gaps, school-readiness gaps, funding gaps, yet still there is another gap that is often overlooked and that is the cultural gap between students and teachers. (www.tolerance.org) When teaching you have to be willing to be open and accepting of others that don't look like you, talk like you or think like you. You will teach students who look the same but have cultural differences. You must also stop yourself from categorizing people solely based on their ethnicity. We can be of the same ethnicity and have different cultural experiences. It's amazing that people are lumped into one pot of this or that. It is possible to be part of a culture and have cultural differences. So to treat everyone the same will create distrust, resentment and cause friction because you're not taking the time to get to know them, but judging them by the thoughts you've already created based on the actions or interactions of others that look like them.

There are many assumptions about students who live in certain areas. What many don't take the time to find out is that there are many professional, financially stable families living in the neighborhoods of those who are living in poverty. Many have been there through several generations, the homes are paid for and the elders refuse to move because they worked to make it their own. Being in a certain area does not dictate who or what you are.

When we embrace cultural differences, differences in general, we open ourselves up to so much. We're able to learn from those who have experienced it or live it first-hand, which can teach us something we never knew, as well as enlighten our previous thoughts or misconceptions. When you close your mind to learning or having the belief that you know all you need to know, you have just become a dangerous person, especially if you fill the role of educator. It will make engaging others that much more difficult, especially those who are less experienced in life.

Each school has a different culture based on the student make up, the community in which it is located and the Principal's way of running the school. No two schools will function alike. I have been in very large schools with 1200-1500 students that were welcoming, serene when you entered, very little if any noise, no students out of class when they shouldn't have been, a tidy building and helpful staff. I have also been to buildings with 700-800 students with total chaos when you enter the door, staff talking inappropriately with students, students doing what they choose without redirection. School culture is set at the beginning the school year with expectations, consistency, follow through and fairness. It is important as educators to band together and follow the school rules and not allowing every incident to have its own set of rules.

When students realize that fairness is not across the board it creates havoc within the building as a whole. And they will remind you of what happened with someone else in the same situation. Saying, "that was different" will only cause them to feel that they are not receiving the same treatment, despite what may have been done behind closed doors with that student. They will always comment on what they see. We all know that perception is reality for many. And this is the case for many students.

School culture may also resonate by the ethnicity of the students in the building. I was in a high school where the majority of the students were Hispanic. My first year there I approached one of the students about her attire and she told me, "you tripping." After multiple students entered the room with similar attire I had to wonder if she was correct. I was being biased about their clothing and when I realized it I talked to them openly to apologize because I had learned something that day about their culture, which I assumed because of what they were wearing. This gave me the opportunity to learn from them and understand things that I didn't know about Hispanics. We went on to build great relationships because I was big enough to admit that I had been wrong about them. They opened up to me throughout the year for advice and would just spend time with me to talk.

I do not believe that anyone is better than the next because our differences are what make us unique and should be adorned. There is so much animosity in the world today regarding race, culture, ethnicity, entitlement and other things that make us different. It should not sway the way you as a teacher interact with your students. They all should receive the same passion despite their skin color or ethnicity. We all can learn something from each other if we take the time to listen and get to know the person. Relationships should be built on character and personality and not perceptions and assumptions.

Donna Burrell

Chapter 6: Master the Craft

Continue to Learn

Once you've received your teaching assignment and if you are unfamiliar with the school, contact the school to find out if you can visit before the school year begins or ends if you're hired during end of year interviews. Find alternate routes to the school from your home to make sure you know how to get there if there are traffic issues, without wasting too much time. Ask for a tour of the building, preferably by a student. This way you see the building the way the students use it, and not just know the path to your room. Learn where the important rooms are, copy room, two restrooms, cafeteria, library, gymnasium (if you're in a middle or high school), and any other place that is relevant to you working in that building.

Request a mentor, to be partnered with a couple of veteran teachers. Starting with two will help you get different viewpoints. If you realize that you've been partnered with negative Nancy or Debbie downer, it is okay to disconnect from them so that you are not taking in toxicity that they haven't learned to deal with yet. Please do not go in with the mindset that, "I got this" and set yourself and your students up for failure. You are working with lives, not widgets. Teaching can and will be hard so asking for help will not appear as a sign of weakness. Anyone in the field for more than two years can attest to this. Making sure that you're taking care of yourself will help you to continue to be creative and motivated in working with your students.

Reach out to your students for feedback if you have an age group that is able to present you their thoughts on what would help them be successful. It can help you reduce your stress level. I requested feedback about every three or four weeks to ensure that we are all on the same page. This helped me to work on how I was presenting information and engaged with them. It is necessary! I found out things that I didn't know I was doing while I was teaching, nothing harmful, but I was told that I rolled my eyes a lot. I was totally unaware of this. I talked with my classes and we laughed about it. They gave me examples of my wording, my body language and my behaviors toward them. It was great learning experience for me and it helped me evolve into being an educator and not just a teacher. By bringing myself into the classroom, being honest with my students, providing structure (yes, I was labeled as mean) and having high expectations of them and myself, I managed to get students to come to school when they would normally not show.

Be Creative and Have Fun

Whatever you do, do not attempt to reinvent the wheel. There are so many ways to find creative ideas to present your curriculum to engage and motivate your students. Start with your student's interests to be included in the assignments, projects and assessments. What they value will make them get more involved. Also, allow them to choose topics when the opportunity is there, with your approval of course. I know I didn't like being given what to work on when I was in school. Nothing motivated me when it was something that I had no interest in.

There are countless educational sites with lessons that you can tweak to fit what you want to present and teach. Ask other teachers for ideas, as well as products that are sold. Remember, the book should be the foundation and not the end. The technology that we now have access to should be used in class. Keep up with the times and you will be able to keep your students engaged, eager and excited to be in your classes.

Resources

Hawley, Jordan Irvine, & Landa, Culture in the Classroom

https://www.tolerance.org/culture-classroom

Https://lesley.edu/article/six-ways-for-educators-to-avoid-compassion-fatigue

Https://www.tolerance.org/professional-development/democratic-classrooms

Sir Ken Robinson, Changing Education Paradigms (Robinson, 2017, https://www.revisesociology.com/2017/07/30/ken-robinson

About the Author

B. A., Lakeland College
Business Administration

MBA, Cardinal Stritch University

M. S., Cardinal Stritch University
Educational Leadership

#10 Wisconsin Department of Education
Director of Instruction

#51 Wisconsin Department of Instruction
K-12 Principal

Educational Coach-Consultant

Time To Teach ™ Trainer - Student Engagement and Motivation
Certified Life Coach

Author

Missing the Mark: Miseducation of Urban Students
Believe In Yourself

Testimonials

Ms. Burrell is very knowledgeable about the cultural background of all students in the urban setting. Her approach and demeanor is non-threatening which draws students and adults to her. She is self-driven and self-motivated. She always finds strategies that would address the different needs of her students. She's very energetic and an excellent support of organizational leadership. She is always seeking the success of organizations or the system in which she works.

Supervising Principal

One of Ms. Burrell's best skills is her leadership. She takes on leadership roles in instruction and climate challenges. She worked diligently with teachers, administrators and parents to help students succeed. She worked effectively as a school administrator in the urban public school system. Her effective and adaptive leadership skills created confidence in administrators that the school would run smoothly, in instruction and climate, when she was at the helm. Her leadership skills have helped instruction in classrooms.

Supervising Principal

Donna Burrell